Fully known, Fully Free

A JOURNEY TO YOUR TRUE IDENTITY IN CHRIST

JEANNINE

This book is a devotional work based on biblical principles and the author's personal revelations. It is not intended to replace regular Bible study or the counsel of the Holy Spirit.

Special thanks to Mickey Mikolauskas, UK, the artist who shared their work freely on Pixabay, which helped bring the cover of this devotional to life.

First Edition: 2024

INDEX

INTRODUCTION

Welcome to *Fully Known, Fully Free: A Journey to Your True Identity in Christ.*

This journal is not just a devotional - it's an invitation. It is an invitation to discover who you truly are in Christ, not based on what you've done, but on what Jesus already accomplished. Each scripture is followed by a devotional insight with questions for reflection that are designed to help you uncover and discover your God-given identity through the lens of grace and truth.

You are free to explore these pages in any order. This is not a checklist or a 31-day plan - it's a Spirit-led journey. Let the Holy Spirit guide you. Pause where He nudges and linger where He speaks/whispers. Some verses may lead you to weep, others to rejoice, and many to stand taller in the authority that is already yours in Christ.

As you study, meditate, and reflect, I pray that your heart is awakened to these truths: you are fully loved by God, you are fully known by God and you are fully free in Him. May this journal become a place of transformation where you rise in confidence, walking boldly in the identity and authority given to you by the grace of God.

Jeannine

THIS BOOK BELONGS TO

_____

and it is a testimony to your devotion to grow deeper in your relationship with Christ and your identity in Him, to live fully known and fully free, and to walk in the truth of who He says you are.

May every page be a reminder that you are chosen, loved and empowered, and called for such a time as this.

_"How precious also are Your thoughts to me, O God!
How great is the sum of them!"
- Psalm 139:17 (NKJV)_

YOU ARE A NEW CREATION

"Therefore, if anyone is in Christ, he is a new creation; the old has passed away; behold, the new has come." - 2 Corinthians 5:17 (ESV)

You are not a patched-up version of your past - you are brand new. The moment you received Jesus, your old nature died, and you were born again in spirit. The "old you" with all its shame, guilt, and failures was crucified with Christ. That means you're not trying to **become** a new creation - you **already** are one.

But walking in that truth requires a shift in thinking. The world may still try to label you by your past, but God never will. He sees you through the finished work of Jesus - holy, righteous, blameless, and dearly loved.

This isn't about trying harder to change - it's about renewing your mind to who you already are in Christ. The more you believe the truth about your identity, the more your life will naturally reflect it. Transformation begins not with striving, but with seeing.

Reflection Questions:

What "old things" are you still identifying with that Jesus already made new?

_____

_____

_____

_____

How does it change your confidence to know your identity is rooted in Christ, not in performance?

_____

_____

_____

_____

_____

Journal:
Write a declaration that reflects who you are in Christ today. Include any lies you're letting go of and truths you're choosing to believe.

YOU ARE LAVISHLY LOVED

"Behold what manner of love the Father has bestowed on us, that we should be called children of God! Therefore, the world does not know us, because it did not know Him." - 1 John 3:1 (NKJV)

Take a moment and let that first word sink in: **Behold**. It means to stop, to look deeply, to consider with awe. John isn't just making a statement here, he's inviting us into wonder. He's saying, "Don't rush past this. Let it overwhelm you."

The kind of love the Father has **bestowed** (freely given, not earned) is unlike anything the world can offer or comprehend. This love doesn't wait for you to get it right, it's a love that calls you His child the moment you say yes to Jesus. That word **child** isn't just a title - it's your new identity.

You are not a servant trying to earn a place in the household. You are a daughter. This is the reason your Father is delighted in you.

The world might not understand this kind of identity, because it's not based on performance, status, or reputation. It's based on relationship. You are known, chosen, and called His own.

Reflection Questions:

Do you see yourself as a beloved child of God, or are there areas in your life you are still trying to earn His approval?

_____

_____

_____

_____

_____

_____

_____

_____

_____

What changes when you believe that God has already called you His? For example: mindset, feelings, images?

_____

_____

_____

_____

_____

_____

Journal:
Write a letter to your Heavenly Father from the heart of a child who knows they are deeply and securely loved. Let Him speak back to you as you write.

_____

_____

_____

_____

_____

_____

_____

_____

_____

_____

_____

_____

_____

_____

_____

THE GREAT EXCHANGE

"God made Him who had no sin to be sin for us, so that we might become the righteousness of God in Him."
- 2 Corinthians 5:21 (NKJV)

This verse reveals one of the most powerful truths in the gospel: the divine exchange. Jesus, who never sinned - not once - took your sin upon Himself. But He didn't stop there. In return, He gave you His righteousness. Not a lesser version. Not a conditional or borrowed kind. His very own righteousness.

That means today, you're not **trying** to become righteous. You **are** the righteousness of God in Christ - right now. Fully and completely.

Why is knowing this so important? Because when you believe in this truth, it changes everything. You stop approaching God as a beggar and come to Him as a beloved child. You stop striving and start resting. You stop hiding in shame and begin walking in freedom.

This righteousness isn't based on your performance. It's based on your position - **in Him**. The more you see yourself through this lens of **"I am already righteous"**, the more your thoughts, actions, and decisions will align with your true identity.

Reflection Questions:

How do you see yourself, as a sinner trying to be good, or as someone already made righteous in Christ.

_____

_____

_____

_____

_____

_____

_____

How would your confidence, prayer life, or relationships change if you believed you were truly righteous?

_____

_____

_____

_____

Journal:
Write a declaration of your righteousness in Christ. Let it be a reminder that you are no longer defined by your past, but by Jesus' perfect righteousness within you.

_____

_____

_____

_____

_____

_____

_____

_____

_____

_____

_____

_____

_____

_____

GRACE IS THE GIFT

"For by grace you have been saved through faith, and that not of yourselves; it is the gift of God." - **Ephesians 2:8**

Grace is not a reward. It's not a paycheck for good behavior, perfect church attendance, or spiritual effort. Grace is a **gift** - freely given, **never** earned. And the moment you stop trying to qualify for it is the moment you begin to experience its power.

So many believers live under the weight of "doing more" to be right with God. But salvation didn't start with you, and it doesn't rest on you now. God's grace initiated it, and faith simply receives what grace has already made available.

This truth sets you free from the performance trap. You no longer have to prove yourself to God - Jesus already did. You can rest, not strive. Receive, not earn. Live from a place of acceptance, not for it.

Here's the beautiful part: the more you believe that grace is enough, the more your life will naturally reflect it. Grace doesn't produce laziness. It produces love, gratitude, and transformation from the inside out.

Reflection Questions:

What are you working for that grace has already made yours?

_____

_____

_____

_____

How does seeing grace as a gift change how you relate to God?

_____

_____

_____

_____

Journal:
Write a prayer of gratitude for God's unearned, undeserved grace in your life. Let it be a moment to release striving and embrace rest.

_____

_____

_____

_____

_____

_____

_____

_____

_____

_____

_____

_____

_____

_____

_____

_____

_____

_____

_____

_____

_____

_____

YOU ARE AN HEIR OF GOD

"Now if we are children, then we are heirs - heirs of God and co-heirs with Christ." - Romans 8:17 (NIV)

You're not just a believer - you're family. You're not just forgiven - you're adopted. As a child of God, you are an **heir** of everything your Father has - not someday in heaven, but right now, in Christ.

This verse declares something radical: you are a joint heir with Jesus. That means what belongs to Him has been made available to you - not because you've earned it, but because grace placed you in His family.

Healing, peace, righteousness, authority, wisdom, purpose - all of it is part of your inheritance. It's not locked away in some far-off future. The moment you received Christ you stepped into this inheritance. But like any heir, you need to know what's yours in order to walk in the fullness of it.

Yes, life may bring challenges. Paul speaks of suffering here not as punishment, but as part of living in a fallen world while carrying the light of Christ. Yet even in hardship, your position doesn't change. **You are still an heir**.

Your Father is not holding back from you. He's inviting you to receive, to believe, and to live from the fullness of what Jesus died to give.

Reflection Questions:

How does seeing yourself as a joint heir with Christ challenge the belief that you have to earn your place in God's family?

_____

_____

_____

_____

_____

_____

What part of your inheritance do you need to start receiving by faith today?

_____

_____

_____

_____

_____

Journal:

Write a declaration as a child of God and joint heir with Christ. Speak it over your life. Let it remind you that you are no longer striving - you're receiving.

_____

_____

_____

_____

_____

_____

_____

_____

_____

_____

_____

_____

_____

_____

Redeemed and forgiven

"In Him we have redemption through His blood, the forgiveness of sins, according to the riches of His grace."
- Ephesians 1:7 (NKJV)

You are not barely forgiven. You are not tolerated. You are fully redeemed. You are completely forgiven - because of His blood, not your performance. This isn't forgiveness on layaway. This is total freedom, purchased in full by the sacrifice of Jesus.

Redemption means to be bought back, rescued or restored. God didn't just cover your sins. He removed them. He didn't just forgive you a little. He forgave you according to the riches of His grace. That means there's no shortage, no limits, and no expiration date on His mercy.

Sometimes, it's hard to believe this when you feel like you've fallen short - again. But this verse anchors you to truth that your forgiveness isn't based on how sorry you are or how good you've been. It's based on Jesus' finished work.

So, when guilt tries to whisper, **"You messed up,"** respond with, **"I'm redeemed."** When shame says, **"You're disqualified,"** remind yourself, **"I've been forgiven - fully and forever."**

You don't have to earn what Jesus already gave. Rest in it. Receive it. And let His grace empower you to walk in freedom.

Reflection Questions:

Are there any areas where guilt still lingers despite God's promise of full forgiveness?

_____

_____

How can knowing you're redeemed change the way you respond to mistakes or regrets?

_____

_____

_____

Journal:
Write a prayer thanking Jesus for your redemption. Release any
lingering shame and step fully into the grace that's already yours.

_____

_____

_____

_____

_____

_____

_____

_____

_____

_____

_____

_____

_____

_____

_____

_____

_____

_____

_____

YOU ARE HIS DWELLING PLACE

"Do you not know that your bodies are temples of the Holy Spirit, who is in you, whom you have received from God?"
- 1 Corinthians 6:19 (NIV)

God isn't distant. He's not watching you from the sky, waiting for you to prove yourself worthy of His presence. The truth is far more powerful and far more intimate. The moment you received Jesus, the Holy Spirit took up residence **within** you.

You don't need to chase after God's presence, it lives in you. You don't need to beg for connection. You've been united. Your body is not just a vessel, it's His temple -chosen, holy, set apart.

This changes everything about how you see yourself. You are not common. You are not random. You are sacred space. The same Spirit that raised Christ from the dead now lives in you, empowering you to live in freedom, righteousness, and boldness.

And here's the grace: even when you don't feel worthy, He remains. Even when you fall short, His Spirit doesn't leave. You are His dwelling place - not because you've perfected your behavior, but because Jesus made you clean.

Reflection Questions:

How does knowing you are God's temple change the way you see yourself and your worth?

_____

_____

_____

What does it mean to you that the Holy Spirit lives within you? How does that truth affect the way you see yourself and your everyday life?

_____

_____

_____

22

Journal:

Write a declaration of reverence and gratitude for the Holy Spirit living inside you. Invite Him to guide, strengthen, and remind you of who you are.

_____

_____

_____

_____

_____

_____

_____

_____

_____

_____

_____

_____

_____

_____

_____

_____

_____

_____

_____

_____

CHOSEN BEFORE TIME

"Just as He chose us in Him before the foundation of the world, that we should be holy and without blame before Him in love."
- Ephesians 1:4 (NKJV)

Before the world began - before your first breath, your first mistake, or your first prayer - God chose you. He did not do so reluctantly nor randomly, but **intentionally**. He saw you, loved you, and set you apart in Christ before you ever had the chance to qualify or disqualify yourself.

That means your identity isn't rooted in what you've done. It's rooted in what He decided. You were wanted. You were planned. You were **positioned** - to be holy and blameless before Him, not by striving, but through His love.

When God looks at you, He doesn't see your flaws or failures. He sees you **in Christ**, covered in grace, clothed in righteousness, completely accepted. This love isn't shallow. It's not based on your performance. It's based on His eternal purpose and unwavering affection.

In a world full of rejection and comparison, this truth anchors your soul: you are chosen. You are fully known. You are deeply loved. You are forever secure.

Reflection Questions:

What does it mean to you that God chose you before the foundation of the world?

_____

_____

_____

_____

_____

_____

_____

In which areas in your life do you still feel the need to earn God's approval?

_____

_____

_____

_____

_____

Journal:
Write a letter to God acknowledging that you are chosen, loved, and accepted. Let it be a reminder to your heart that your identity is not achieved, it's received.

_____

_____

_____

_____

_____

_____

_____

_____

_____

_____

_____

_____

_____

_____

_____

_____

_____

TRULY FREE

"So if the Son sets you free, you will be free indeed."
- John 8:36 (NIV)

Freedom in Christ isn't symbolic - it's real. It's not something we hope for someday in heaven. It's something we are meant to live in right now. When Jesus says you are free, He means **free from shame, free from guilt, free from sin, free from fear, and free from striving.**

This kind of freedom doesn't come from trying harder. It doesn't come from perfect behavior or religious effort. It comes from one thing alone, being made free by the Son.

You may still feel the pull of old habits, the echo of past labels, or the weight of people's opinions. But none of those things define you anymore. You are not bound. You are not stuck. You are not broken beyond repair. You are **free indeed** - fully, completely, irrevocably free.

And when you truly believe this, you'll begin to walk differently - not in fear of failure, but in confidence of grace. You will not work to earn His love, because you already have it. Jesus didn't just open the prison door, He took you by the hand and walked you out.

Reflection Questions:

What areas of your life still feel bound, even though Jesus says you're free?

_____

_____

_____

How would your life change if you believed you were *truly* free today?

_____

_____

_____

_____

Journal:

Write a declaration of freedom. Name the lies or limitations you're releasing and then speak the truth of your identity as someone Jesus has set free.

_____

_____

_____

_____

_____

_____

_____

_____

_____

_____

_____

_____

_____

_____

_____

_____

_____

_____

_____

_____

More than a Conqueror

"Yet in all these things we are more than conquerors through Him who loved us." - Romans 8:37 (NKJV)

This verse doesn't say you're barely getting by. It doesn't say you're a survivor. It boldly declares that you are **more than a conqueror** - not in your own strength, but **through Him who loved you.**

It's easy to feel overwhelmed by life's challenges, trials, disappointments, delays, and even spiritual battles. But Paul wrote this verse not from comfort, but in the midst of hardship. Yet he reminds us that God's love doesn't just help us endure, it empowers us to overcome.

To be more than a conqueror means you don't just win, you win with peace. You overcome with joy. You go through the storm and you come out stronger, not because of your might, but because of the One who loves you and never leaves your side.

His love doesn't guarantee a life without pressure, but it does guarantee that the **pressure won't defeat you**. You're not trying to achieve victory. You're standing in the victory Jesus already secured. That's your identity: victorious, equipped, and deeply loved.

Reflection Questions:

Where in your life do you need to shift from a defeated mindset to a conqueror's perspective?

_____

_____

_____

How does God's love empower you to face what's in front of you?

_____

_____

_____

_____

Journal:

Write a bold declaration: *"I am more than a conqueror in..."* and add any area you feel like you have not overcome yet. Let it be a reminder that no matter what you're walking through, you're walking in victory because Jesus already won.

_____

_____

_____

_____

_____

_____

_____

_____

_____

_____

_____

_____

_____

_____

_____

_____

_____

_____

_____

_____

_____

_____

COMPLETE IN HIM

"For you died, and your life is hidden with Christ in God."
- Colossians 3:3 (NKJV)

There is nothing missing in you. There is nothing broken. There is nothing lacking. In Christ, you are **complete**. That means you don't need to chase approval, affirmation, or validation from the world to feel whole. Jesus has already filled every gap with Himself.

This kind of completeness doesn't come from achievements, relationships, titles, or outward perfection. It comes from being **in Him**. The One who rules over all power and authority chose to make His fullness dwell in you. Because He lacks nothing, you lack nothing.

The enemy would love for you to believe you're not enough, that you need to earn your worth, that something still needs to be "fixed" before you can be fully used by God. But this verse silences that lie. You are not being made more complete, **you are complete**, right now, in Him.

That doesn't mean you stop growing. It means you grow from fullness, not from emptiness. You live from identity, not for it.

Reflection Questions:

In which areas in your life have you've been striving to become what God already says you are?

_____

_____

_____

_____

How does knowing you're complete in Christ shift the way you see yourself today?

_____

_____

_____

_____

Journal:

Write a prayer of confidence, declaring that you are whole and complete in Jesus. Ask the Holy Spirit to reveal any area where you've been living like something is missing and invite His truth to fill that space.

_____

_____

_____

_____

_____

_____

_____

_____

_____

_____

_____

_____

_____

_____

_____

_____

_____

_____

You are the Salt of the Earth

"You are the salt of the earth; but if the salt loses its flavor, how shall it be seasoned? It is then good for nothing but to be thrown out and trampled underfoot by men." - Matthew 5:13 (NKJV)

Jesus didn't say you **might become** salt. He said you **are** the salt of the earth. That's identity, not assignment. Your presence matters. Anchored in Christ, your life preserves truth, adds flavor, and carries influence beyond what you can see.

Salt purifies, preserves, and awakens. In the same way, your words carry truth, your kindness reflects grace, and your faith helps preserve a broken world. You weren't meant to blend in. **You were made to make a difference.**

Jesus gives a gentle warning: if salt loses its flavor, it loses its effectiveness. You don't lose your value, but you can forget your purpose. This verse calls you back to identity, to authenticity, and to grace-filled influence.

You don't need a spotlight to make an impact, just the confidence to live from who you already are in Him.

Reflection Questions:

What might be holding you back from fully walking in the influence and purpose God designed you for?

_____

_____

_____

_____

How can you or are you using the influence and purpose God has placed in you to impact the world around you?

_____

_____

_____

Journal:

Write a prayer asking the Lord to keep you "salty" - full of grace, truth, and boldness. Declare that you will live from your identity and be a preserving influence in your world.

_____

_____

_____

_____

_____

_____

_____

_____

_____

_____

_____

_____

_____

_____

_____

_____

_____

_____

_____

_____

YOU BELONG TO THE TRUE GOD

"And we [have seen and] know [positively] that the Son of God has [actually] come to this world and has given us understanding and insight [progressively] to perceive [recognize] and come to know better and more clearly Him Who is true; and we are in Him Who is true - in His Son Jesus Christ (the Messiah). This [Man] is the true God and Life eternal." - 1 John 5:20 AMPC

This verse is a gentle yet powerful reminder: you're not guessing your way through faith, you've been given understanding. You can know God personally and intimately, not just know about Him.

As you spend time in the Word and with the Holy Spirit, you begin to see more clearly who God is and who you are in Him. You're not stumbling in darkness. Jesus has already brought you into the light and given you insight to live from that place of knowing.

Here's the power in it: you are in Him who is true. Your identity isn't rooted in feelings, the past, or others' opinions. It's rooted in Christ, the One who is eternal life. The more you grow in that truth, the more confident and free you become.

This isn't head knowledge, it's heart revelation. You are in union with the True God. That truth brings clarity, peace, and unshakable stability.

Reflection Questions:

How does knowing you are in union with the One who is true shape the way you approach your day-to-day life?

_____

_____

_____

What "truths" have you believed about God or yourself that need to be replaced with what the Word says?

_____

_____

_____

Journal:

Write a declaration of what you know to be true about who God is and what that means for your identity. Thank Him for the insight He continues to give you through His Spirit.

_____

_____

_____

_____

_____

_____

_____

_____

_____

_____

_____

_____

_____

_____

_____

_____

_____

_____

_____

_____

_____

Life is in the Son

"And this is the testimony: that God has given us eternal life, and this life is in His Son. He who has the Son has life; he who does not have the Son of God does not have life." - 1 John 5:11–12 (NKJV)

This passage isn't a mystery, it's a testimony. It's a bold declaration from heaven. Eternal life is a gift, and that life is found in one place only - in the Son. It is not found not in striving, not in accomplishments, and not even in good intentions. Life is in Him.

This life isn't just about going to heaven one day. **It's about living in the fullness of God's nature now**. Eternal life begins the moment you receive Jesus as Lord. His peace becomes your peace. His joy becomes your strength. His righteousness becomes your foundation.

You don't have to wonder if you're "good enough" to earn this life. If you have the Son, you have life. That's identity. That's security. That's rest.

And the reverse is also clear: "he who does not have the Son... does not have life." This is not declaring a punishment but rather a spiritual reality. Jesus is the only source. The beautiful truth is, He has made Himself fully available to anyone who says "Yes".

So, walk in that assurance today. You have the Son. You have life. You do not have a lesser version. You are not on a waiting list. You have life now.

Reflection Questions:

What would shift in your daily life if you lived fully aware that eternal life is already yours in Christ?

_____

_____

_____

_____

_____

_____

What areas of your life need to come into alignment with the truth that you already possess His life?

_____

_____

_____

_____

Journal:

"I have the Son. I have life." Speak it out loud. Meditate on it. Let it reshape how you think, respond, and walk through your day. What is the Holy Spirit to showing you how to apply that truth today?

_____

_____

_____

_____

_____

_____

_____

_____

_____

_____

_____

_____

_____

_____

_____

_____

_____

LOVE MADE VISIBLE

"In this the love of God was manifested toward us, that God has sent His only begotten Son into the world, that we might live through Him." - 1 John 4:9

Love isn't just a feeling God has toward you. It's a reality He demonstrated. He didn't love from a distance. He sent His Son not out of obligation, but out of overflowing affection. This wasn't just about rescuing you. It was about restoring you to life through Him.

Jesus coming to earth is the greatest love story ever told, and you are the reason He came. God's love was not abstract. It was **manifested** - revealed, proven, embodied - in the person of Jesus Christ. Every word He spoke, every healing He performed, every drop of blood He shed was a loud declaration: **You are deeply loved**.

Now, because of Him, you don't just survive - **you live**. You live through His Spirit, His strength, and His unshakable grace. The life you now live isn't powered by your own willpower. It flows from the One who loves you perfectly and completely.

This is the anchor of your identity: you are loved beyond measure - not because you earned it, but because God is love, and He has **manifested** that love personally to you.

Reflection Questions:

Do you truly believe God's love was demonstrated *for you* personally and in what ways have you seen it?

_____

_____

_____

_____

_____

_____

_____

How can you live today as someone deeply loved by God?

_____

_____

_____

_____

_____

Journal:
Write a personal thank-you letter to God for sending Jesus - not just to save you, but so that you could truly _live_ through Him.

_____

_____

_____

_____

_____

_____

_____

_____

_____

_____

_____

_____

_____

_____

HE ABIDES IN YOU

"Now he who keeps His commandments abides in Him, and He in him. And by this we know that He abides in us, by the Spirit whom He has given us"- 1 John 3:24 (NKJV)

God didn't save you just to leave you. He **abides in you.** That means He has taken up permanent residence within your heart. You don't need to chase after His presence. You carry it. His Spirit is not a visitor. He's your Helper, your Comforter, your constant Companion.

This verse is a beautiful reminder of both assurance and intimacy. You know that God abides in you, not because of feelings or circumstances, but because of the Spirit He gave you. His Spirit bears witness within you, guiding you, reminding you that you belong to Him.

"But what about keeping His commandments?" you may ask. It's not a legalistic checklist. It's the natural result of living in union with Him. When you're abiding in Christ, love becomes your motivation. Obedience flows from identity, not obligation.

You're not doing life for God. You're doing life **with** God. Every moment, every decision, every breath is shared with the One who calls you His dwelling place.

Reflection Questions:

In what ways have you recognized the Holy Spirit's presence as evidence of God abiding in you?

_____

_____

_____

_____

_____

_____

_____

How can you become more aware of His voice and presence in your everyday life?

_____

_____

_____

_____

_____

_____

Journal:

Write a personal reflection thanking the Holy Spirit for abiding in you. Ask Him to make you more aware of His presence and to deepen your intimacy with the Father.

_____

_____

_____

_____

_____

_____

_____

_____

_____

_____

_____

_____

WALK LIKE JESUS

"He who says he abides in Him ought himself also to walk just as He walked." - 1 John 2:6 (NKJV)

This verse can feel like a high standard - and it is. But it's not a demand to strive harder. It's an invitation to **live from the same place Jesus lived**: union with the Father, led by the Spirit, grounded in love.

To walk as Jesus walked isn't about perfectly mimicking every external behavior. It's about **walking in the same heart posture** - resting in the Father's love, fully surrendered, grace-empowered, and Spirit-filled.

You can walk as He walked because you're **abiding** in Him. The same Spirit that was in Jesus is now in you. And the more you recognize your identity in Him, the more naturally your life begins to reflect His nature.

This walk is not performance-driven. It's presence-driven. It's not about "trying" to be like Jesus. It's about **believing** that you already carry His nature inside you and letting that truth shape your every step.

Reflection Questions:

Which areas in your life have you been trying to act like Jesus without first abiding in Him?

_____

_____

_____

_____

_____

_____

_____

_____

_____

What would it look like to walk from union, not effort?

_____

_____

_____

_____

_____

Journal:
Write a prayer asking the Holy Spirit to help you walk like Jesus - not in your own strength, but in grace and dependence. Surrender your steps to Him today.

_____

_____

_____

_____

_____

_____

_____

_____

_____

_____

_____

_____

_____

_____

_____

_____

HIS LOVE PERFECTED IN YOU

"But he who keeps (treasures) His Word [who bears in mind His precepts who observes His message in its entirety], truly in him has the love of and for God been perfected (completed, reached maturity). By this we may perceive (know, recognize, and be sure) that we are in Him." - 1 John 2:5 (AMPC)

To keep God's Word isn't just about obedience, it's about treasuring it, holding it close, letting it shape your heart, renew your mind, and anchor your decisions. When you treat His Word as precious, something begins to happen inside you. His love grows deeper, stronger, and more mature in you.

This verse speaks of perfected love - not flawless performance, but love that's growing into its full expression. It speaks of a love that's not just something you receive from God, but something that begins to flow back to Him and through you to others. It's a maturing love that transforms how you think, how you speak, and how you respond to the world around you.

The Word of God isn't just information. It's transformation. As you meditate on it, reflect on it, and walk in it, you begin to see who God really is and, just as powerfully, who you really are in Him.

You don't need to question whether you're truly "in Him." This verse gives you a simple confirmation: the one who treasures His Word and lets it shape their life can be sure they are in Him. You can know that His love is taking root and growing strong in you - day by day, word by word.

Reflection Questions:

Are you treasuring God's Word, or simply reading it? How can you invite His Word to go deeper?

_____

_____

_____

_____

_____

In what ways have you seen His love maturing in your life?

_____

_____

_____

_____

_____

Journal:

Write a prayer asking God to perfect His love in you through His Word. Commit to treasuring His voice and letting His truth shape your identity more deeply each day.

_____

_____

_____

_____

_____

_____

_____

_____

_____

_____

_____

_____

_____

_____

_____

LIVING FOR THE WILL OF GOD

"Therefore, since Christ suffered for us in the flesh, arm yourselves also with the same mind, for he who has suffered in the flesh has ceased from sin, that he no longer should live the rest of his time in the flesh for the lusts of men, but for the will of God."
- 1 Peter 4:1-2 (NKJV)

Jesus didn't just die for your sin. He modeled a life fully surrendered to the will of God. His suffering wasn't just redemptive, it was also instructional. It showed us how to live with a mindset that values obedience over comfort, purpose over pleasure, and truth over convenience.

Peter encourages you to arm yourself with this same mind, not out of fear but from a place of resolve, to make a decision to let the finished work of Jesus change how you think and how you live. The more deeply you know who you are in Christ, the less appeal sin holds over you. Grace doesn't excuse sin. **It empowers you to live free from it.**

You're not a slave to your old desires anymore. You're not defined by your past or pulled around by your emotions. You've been given a new nature, and with it comes a new desire: to live for God's will.

This is not about earning His approval. **You already have it.** It's about walking in the freedom that comes from being aligned with His purpose and heart for your life.

Reflection Questions:

Where do you sense God calling you to step out of ease and into deeper purpose with Him?

_____

_____

_____

_____

_____

_____

What does it look like for you to arm your mind with the same mindset as Christ?

_____

_____

_____

_____

_____

Journal:

Write a prayer of surrender, committing your desires, plans, and daily choices to the will of God. Ask the Holy Spirit to renew your mind and help you walk in this mindset of grace-driven obedience.

_____

_____

_____

_____

_____

_____

_____

_____

_____

_____

_____

_____

_____

_____

_____

_____

_____

EQUIPPED FOR EVERY GOOD THING

"Now may the God of peace who brought up our Lord Jesus from the dead, that great Shepherd of the sheep, through the blood of the everlasting covenant, [21] make you complete in every good work to do His will, working in you what is well pleasing in His sight, through Jesus Christ, to whom be glory forever and ever. Amen." - **Hebrews 13:20-21 (NKJV)**

You are not left to figure life out on your own. The same God who raised Jesus from the dead, the same Shepherd who laid down His life for you, is the One working **in you** - equipping you, completing you, empowering you.

These verses are more than a prayer. They are a powerful promise: God Himself is at work in you. He's not asking you to muster up strength or prove your worth. He's working what is well **pleasing in His sight** through Christ living in you. That means even your desire to do His will comes from Him. You're not alone in this journey.

And notice this: it's all through the blood of the **everlasting covenant**. His covenant with you is not fragile or temporary. It's eternal, sealed in grace, and backed by the finished work of Jesus.

You are **complete in Him**, equipped for every good thing - not because you've perfected your behavior, but because He is faithfully working in you, shaping you into the fullness of who you are in Christ.

Reflection Questions:

How do you see God actively working *in* you - not just around you or for you, but within your heart, desires, and decisions?

_____

_____

_____

_____

_____

_____

What good works is He inviting you into right now, and how can you trust Him to equip you for them?

_____

_____

_____

_____

_____

Journal:

Write a prayer thanking God for being your Shepherd and your strength. Invite Him to continue working in your heart and life as you surrender to His will, knowing He equips you for every good thing.

_____

_____

_____

_____

_____

_____

_____

_____

_____

_____

_____

_____

_____

_____

EQUIPPED BY THE WORD

"All scripture is given by inspiration of God, and is profitable for doctrine, for reproof, for correction, for instruction in righteousness, that the man of God may be complete, thoroughly equipped for every good work." - **2 Timothy 3:16-17 (NKJV)**

The Bible isn't just a book. It's God-breathed. Every word carries His heart, His wisdom, and His desire for you to walk in truth, identity, and purpose. Scripture isn't meant to weigh you down with rules. It's meant to **build you up,** to equip you for every good work He's called you to.

When you open the Word, you're not reading to earn approval, you're discovering who you already are. The Word teaches you what's true, corrects what doesn't align with your identity in Christ, and lovingly trains you in righteousness, not to shame you, but to **complete** you.

God's Word is your spiritual mirror. It reminds you that you're righteous, loved, empowered, and equipped. As you continue to soak in His truth, you begin to live from a place of confidence, not because you have all the answers, but because you know the One who does.

You don't need to be perfect to be powerful. You simply need to stay rooted in the Word, letting it shape your heart, renew your mind, and guide your steps.

Reflection Questions:

How can you allow God's Word to train and equip you today?

_____

_____

_____

_____

_____

_____

_____

Are you approaching the Bible as a list of rules, or as a tool for transformation?

_____

_____

_____

_____

_____

Journal:

Write a prayer of commitment to stay in the Word - not out of duty, but out of desire to grow in grace and be thoroughly equipped for the life God has called you to live.

_____

_____

_____

_____

_____

_____

_____

_____

_____

_____

_____

_____

_____

_____

_____

_____

BOLD, LOVING, AND SELF-CONTROLLED

"For God did not give us a spirit of timidity (of cowardice, of craven and cringing and fawning fear), but [He has given us a spirit] of power and of love and of calm and well-balanced mind and discipline and self-control." - 2 Timothy 1:7 (AMPC)

Fear may show up, but it doesn't come from God. That means you don't have to accept it, live under it, or make decisions from it. You've been given a different spirit - **one of power, love, and a well-balanced, disciplined mind.**

This isn't about personality or confidence. It's about the Holy Spirit alive in you. His power strengthens you. His love grounds you. His wisdom steadies your lhoughts and emotions. You've been equipped to live boldly and peacefully at the same time.

When fear tries to speak, remind yourself: it's not your voice and it's not your inheritance. Fear is not your identity. You don't have to strive to be fearless. You already **have** the Spirit of power. All you need to do is agree with who God says you are.

You are not timid. You are not ruled by emotion. You are calm, clear-minded, and full of love and strength - because He lives in you.

Reflection Questions:

What fears or thoughts are you holding onto that God didn't give you?

_____

_____

_____

_____

_____

_____

_____

How can you begin to respond today with power, love, and a sound mind?

_____

_____

_____

_____

_____

Journal:

Write a declaration that begins with: "God did not give me a spirit of fear..." and then speak life over your thoughts, your emotions, and your identity in Christ.

_____

_____

_____

_____

_____

_____

_____

_____

_____

_____

_____

_____

_____

_____

_____

A Life Aligned with His Will

"Rejoice always, pray without ceasing, in everything give thanks; for this is the will of God in Christ Jesus for you."
- 1 Thessalonians 5:16-18 (NKJV)

Sometimes we overcomplicate the will of God. We chase answers, direction, and clarity, Yet here, God gently reveals His heart: **live rejoicing, stay in communion with Him, and be thankful in all things.** This isn't a list of impossible expectations. It's an invitation to live from your new identity.

Joy isn't based on circumstances. It flows from knowing you are loved, accepted, and secure in Christ. Prayer doesn't have to be long or formal. It's simply staying connected with your Father throughout the day. It shifts your perspective from what's missing to the abundance of His presence and provision.

These aren't religious duties. They're grace-powered rhythms that keep your heart anchored in truth. The beauty is, **they're possible**, not because of your effort, but because of Who lives in you.

This kind of life is a witness. It shines in a weary world. It reflects a heart fully alive in Christ.

Reflection Questions:

Which of these three practices - rejoicing, praying, or giving thanks - do you need to realign with today?

_____

_____

_____

_____

How can you build small rhythms into your day to live from a place of connection and gratitude?

_____

_____

_____

Journal:
Write a short gratitude list, then follow it with a simple, honest prayer. End by declaring joy over your heart, regardless of how things look, because your life is hidden in Christ.

_____

_____

_____

_____

_____

_____

_____

_____

_____

_____

_____

_____

_____

_____

_____

_____

_____

_____

_____

_____

_____

POSITIONED IN POWER

"Therefore, submit to God. Resist the devil and he will flee from you."
- James 4:7 (NKJV),

This verse isn't a threat, it's a strategy. It reminds you that spiritual authority flows from spiritual alignment. When you submit to God, you're not giving up freedom, you're stepping into power.

Submission here is not about control or punishment. It's about **agreement**. It's saying yes to God's truth, His Word, His grace, and His Spirit. From this place of agreement, you become equipped to resist every lie, temptation, or attack of the enemy.

The enemy wants you to think you're powerless. But the moment you resist - standing in your identity, standing in the Word, standing in Christ - he **must flee**, not because of how loud you shout, but because of **Who lives in you**.

You're not fighting for victory. You're standing in victory. Submitting to God positions your heart, mind, and voice to enforce what's already yours in Jesus.

Reflection Questions:

Are there any thoughts, habits, or attitudes the Holy Spirit is highlighting that need to be realigned with God's Word?

_____

_____

_____

_____

What lies has the enemy been whispering to you that you now choose to resist?

_____

_____

_____

_____

Journal:

Write a declaration of surrender to God, followed by a bold statement of resistance to anything the enemy has tried to use against you. Speak from your place of authority, knowing the devil *will* flee.

_____

_____

_____

_____

_____

_____

_____

_____

_____

_____

_____

_____

_____

_____

_____

_____

_____

_____

_____

Come Boldly

"Let us then with confidence draw near to the throne of grace, that we may receive mercy and find grace to help in time of need."
- Hebrews 4:16 (ESV)

God's throne is not one of judgment for those in Christ. It is a **throne of grace**. You don't approach with fear or hesitation. You come boldly, confidently, like a daughter who knows she belongs, not because you've done everything right, but because **Jesus already has.**

This verse doesn't say you might receive mercy. It says you **will.** It doesn't say grace is given sparingly. It says it's given **exactly when you need it in abundance.** In moments of weakness, weariness, or failure, God doesn't withdraw. He invites you closer.

Coming boldly isn't arrogance. It's faith. It's believing that because of Jesus, there's nothing standing between you and your Father. You are welcome. You are wanted. You are covered in grace.

This kind of access changes how you pray, how you walk, and how you see yourself. You're not an outsider knocking. You're a child entering your Father's presence with open hands and full assurance.

Reflection Questions:

Identify moments in your life when you hold back from God, thinking He's disappointed in you?

_____

_____

_____

_____

_____

_____

_____

How can you make coming boldly to the throne a regular rhythm in your life?

_____

_____

_____

_____

_____

Journal:

Write a personal prayer approaching the throne of grace. Don't filter your thoughts. Just come honestly. Receive mercy, receive grace, and rest in His presence.

_____

_____

_____

_____

_____

_____

_____

_____

_____

_____

_____

_____

_____

_____

Transferred into Light

"He has delivered us from the power of darkness and conveyed us into the kingdom of the Son of His love." - Colossians 1:13 (NKJV)

You are no longer under the authority of darkness. You've been delivered, rescued, removed, and transferred. You now live in a new kingdom, one ruled not by fear or shame, but by love. And not just any love, but the love of the Son.

This wasn't a gradual shift. It was instant. The moment you believed in Christ, your entire position changed. You were taken out of bondage and placed into belonging. You are not trying to escape darkness. You've already been brought into the light.

This verse reminds you that you live under a new system, a kingdom where grace reigns. Where identity is rooted in Jesus, not your mistakes. Where you don't strive for approval. You stand in it.

The enemy may try to convince you that you're still bound, but the truth is clear: you've been transferred. His lies hold no legal ground. You're no longer a citizen of fear, but of faith. You're not a prisoner, but a child of the King.

Reflection Questions:

What areas in your life do you feel like someone living under the weight of darkness?

_____

_____

_____

_____

Where do you see evidence of God's light at work in your life - bringing clarity, freedom, or growth?

_____

_____

_____

_____

Journal:

Write a declaration of where you now live: in the kingdom of the Son of His love. Declare what no longer has power over you and what your new reality in Christ looks like.

_____
_____
_____
_____
_____
_____
_____
_____
_____
_____
_____
_____
_____
_____
_____
_____
_____
_____
_____
_____
_____
_____

Fully Supplied

"And my God shall supply all your need according to His riches in glory by Christ Jesus." **- Philippians 4:19 (NKJV)**

God doesn't meet your needs according to the economy, your effort, or even your expectations. He supplies **according to His riches in glory by Christ Jesus**. That means His provision is abundant, overflowing, and perfectly timed.

This isn't just financial, It's personal. He supplies strength when you're weary, peace when you're anxious, wisdom when you're uncertain, and grace when you feel inadequate. Every need - spirit, soul, and body - is fully known by your Father and completely covered in Christ.

Notice the phrase: **"My God shall supply."** Paul writes this from a place of confidence and relationship. This isn't a distant deity offering help. It's **your God**, your provider, your source, your Shepherd. He's not rationing out blessings. He gives from the overflow of heaven.

You don't need to live in fear of lack. You can live in rest, knowing that your Father sees, cares, and supplies - faithfully.

Reflection Questions:

What needs are you trusting God to supply and which do you still need to entrust to God?

_____

_____

_____

_____

_____

How does this promise shift your perspective on worry or waiting?

_____

_____

_____

Journal:

Write a prayer thanking God for being your provider. List specific needs you're releasing to Him and declare that you trust His supply to be more than enough.

_____

_____

_____

_____

_____

_____

_____

_____

_____

_____

_____

_____

_____

_____

_____

_____

_____

_____

_____

_____

STRENGTHENED IN HIM

"Finally, be strong in the Lord and in the strength of his might."
- Ephesians 6:10 (ESV)

This verse isn't telling you to muster up inner strength or push through in your own power. It's a call to be strong in the Lord, **to draw your strength from His endless supply**, not your own limited reserves.

You weren't created to carry life's battles alone. Your strength comes from abiding in Jesus, from knowing who you are in Him, and from standing in the authority He's given you. His might is not something you earn. It's something you receive and rest in.

"Finally" means this is the foundation before spiritual battle, before responsibility, before facing the day: **know where your strength comes from.** You are not trying to become strong. You are strong because His Spirit lives in you.

This is not about self-effort. This is about **Spirit-empowerment**. When you feel weak, you can still stand, not because of your determination, but because of His strength working in **you and through you**.

Reflection Questions:

In what areas of your life are you tempted to rely on your own strength, and how is God inviting you to lean into His instead?

_____

_____

_____

_____

_____

What would it look like today to live fully aware of His might flowing through you?

_____

_____

_____

Journal:
Write a prayer surrendering your own strength and inviting His power to take over. Declare: "I am strong in the Lord and in the strength of His might!"

_____

_____

_____

_____

_____

_____

_____

_____

_____

_____

_____

_____

_____

_____

_____

_____

_____

_____

_____

_____

_____

_____

_____

REDEEMED AND BLESSED

"Christ has redeemed us from the curse of the law, having become a curse for us (for it is written, 'Cursed is everyone who hangs on a tree'), that the blessing of Abraham might come upon the Gentiles in Christ Jesus, that we might receive the promise of the Spirit through faith." - **Galatians 3:13–14 (NKJV)**

Jesus didn't just forgive your sins. He **redeemed you from the curse.** Every consequence of the law that demanded perfection, every judgment that came from falling short, every generational chain that tried to hold you back - Jesus took it all. He became the curse so you could walk in **the blessing**.

This means You are no longer under condemnation, fear, lack, or spiritual separation. You are under the blessing of Abraham - righteousness by faith, favor, fruitfulness, and the indwelling of the Holy Spirit.

This blessing isn't earned. It's received. The law said, "Do this and live." Grace says, "Believe, and it's already yours." Jesus fulfilled the law so that, through faith, you can receive the promise of the Spirit - His presence, power, and guidance within you.

You don't have to strive for the blessing. You are the blessed. The more you believe it, the more you'll walk in it.

Reflection Questions:

How is the truth of your freedom from the curse shaping your mindset, your choices, and your confidence today?

_____

_____

_____

_____

_____

_____

_____

What promise of the Spirit are you choosing to receive and walk in today?

_____

_____

_____

_____

_____

Journal:

Write a declaration thanking Jesus for redeeming you from the curse. List the blessings you're believing and receiving by faith as a daughter of the promise.

_____

_____

_____

_____

_____

_____

_____

_____

_____

_____

_____

_____

_____

_____

_____

_____

Established, Anointed, and Sealed

"Now He who establishes us with you in Christ and has anointed us in God, who also has sealed us and given us the Spirit in our hearts as a guarantee." - 2 Corinthians 1:21–22 (NKJV)

These verses are packed with identity truth: **You are established. You are anointed.** You are sealed, **not by your effort,** but by God Himself.

To be **established** means God has planted you securely in Christ. You're not shaky or uncertain, you're rooted. Your position in Him is settled. You're not trying to find your place in the Kingdom. You've already been placed.

To be **anointed** means you've been set apart and empowered for purpose. Anointing is not reserved for the "spiritual elite". It's a mark of God's presence on your life. You carry His Spirit, His authority, and His calling wherever you go.

To be **sealed** means God has claimed you as His own. The Holy Spirit within you is your guarantee - your divine proof of belonging, inheritance, and eternal security. It's God's way of saying, **"She's mine, and nothing can change that."**

You don't have to question whether you're qualified, chosen, or accepted. God has done all the establishing, anointing, and sealing. Your part is to simply believe it and walk in it.

Reflection Questions:

Which truth stands out to you most today: being established, anointed, or sealed?

_____

_____

_____

_____

_____

_____

How does this promise shift the way you view your daily life and purpose?

_____

_____

_____

_____

Journal:

Write a declaration that begins: "I am established, anointed, and sealed by God and because of that..." Let it settle in your heart and silence any voice that says you're not enough.

_____

_____

_____

_____

_____

_____

_____

_____

_____

_____

_____

_____

_____

GOD'S CO-WORKER

"For we are God's fellow workers; you are God's field, you are God's building." - 1 Corinthians 3:9 (NKJV)

You are not working for God. You are working **with** Him. You are His fellow worker, His partner, His vessel. That changes everything. You're not striving for significance. You've been invited into a divine collaboration.

God doesn't need you to build His Kingdom, but He **wants** you. He delights in partnering with His children to bring heaven to earth. Whether through your words, your work, your creativity, or your relationships, you are part of His eternal plan.

Paul also says you are God's **field** and **building**. That means you are both the place where God works and the one He works through. He is cultivating growth in you while also building something through your life that will bear fruit for generations.

This is not about pressure. It's about purpose. Your life matters because you belong to God, and He has chosen to work through you. The same grace that saves you is the grace that empowers you to co-labor with Him.

Reflection Questions:

How does seeing yourself as God's fellow worker change the way you approach your day?

_____

_____

_____

_____

In which areas of your life have you've been striving alone instead of partnering with Him?

_____

_____

_____

Journal:

Write a prayer of partnership. Invite God into your work, your plans, your thoughts, and your daily rhythms. Declare, "I am God's co-worker, and I trust Him to work in me and through me."

_____

_____

_____

_____

_____

_____

_____

_____

_____

_____

_____

_____

_____

_____

_____

_____

_____

_____

_____

_____

_____

_____

PEACE WITH GOD

"Therefore, having been justified by faith, we have peace with God through our Lord Jesus Christ." - Romans 5:1 (NKJV)

You are not in a battle with God. You are not on probation, waiting for Him to decide if you're good enough. You have been **justified** - declared righteous - by faith in Jesus. Because of that, you now live in a state of **peace** with God.

This peace isn't temporary. It's not based on your behavior, emotions, or circumstances. It's based on a legal, spiritual reality: the war is over. The distance is gone. The debt is paid. You've been brought near, fully accepted, and permanently reconciled.

So many believers are still trying to earn peace with God, but this verse gently reminds you: **you already have it.** You can rest, breathe, and approach Him with confidence. The Prince of Peace lives in you and His finished work has secured your standing forever.

Let that peace rule in your heart. Let it silence fear, shame, and striving. Let it anchor you when life feels unstable. You are not working for peace. You are living from it.

Reflection Questions:

What thoughts, feelings, or habits reveal whether you're resting in peace with God or still trying to earn what He's already given?

_____

_____

_____

_____

How can this truth shape the way you pray, worship, and relate to Him today?

_____

_____

_____

_____

Journal:
Write a declaration: "Because of Jesus, I have peace with God." Let it settle deep in your spirit as a reminder that you are fully accepted and forever loved.

_____

_____

_____

_____

_____

_____

_____

_____

_____

_____

_____

_____

_____

_____

_____

_____

_____

_____

BORN TO OVERCOME

"For whatever is born of God overcomes the world. And this is the victory that has overcome the world - our faith." - 1 John 5:4 (NKJV)

You weren't born again to be a victim of the world. You were born to **overcome** it. This verse doesn't say you might overcome or that you'll eventually get the victory. **It says your very spiritual DNA is wired for victory.**

If you are born of God - and you are - then overcoming is not something you chase. It's who you are. The world may throw trials, pressures, temptations, and lies your way, but none of them can override the **power of Christ within you.** Your faith, not your feelings, is the proof and pathway to victory.

Faith isn't about ignoring reality - it's about standing on a **higher** reality: what God has said, what Christ has done, and who you are in Him. When you believe that truth, you rise above circumstances instead of being crushed by them.

You don't overcome by striving. **You overcome by believing.** And faith in Jesus is what gives you access to the overcoming life He already won.

Reflection Questions:

In what areas of your life do you need to stop striving and start standing in faith?

_____

_____

_____

_____

What would change if you truly believed you were born to overcome?

_____

_____

_____

Journal:

Write a declaration of victory rooted in your identity. Begin with: "Because I am born of God, I overcome..." and finish it with truth that silences fear and activates faith.

_____

_____

_____

_____

_____

_____

_____

_____

_____

_____

_____

_____

_____

_____

_____

_____

_____

_____

_____

_____

_____

ALL HIS PROMISES ARE YES

"For all the promises of God in Him are Yes, and in Him Amen, to the glory of God through us." **- 2 Corinthians 1:20 (NKJV)**

God's promises aren't shaky, vague, or reserved for "special" people. In Christ, every promise He's ever made now carries a bold, unwavering "**Yes**." These promises are not "maybe," not "someday", but yes and amen.

Because you are in Christ, God's "yes" is your inheritance. Every word of healing, provision, peace, purpose, righteousness, and redemption is already affirmed in Him. You don't have to beg for what's been promised. **You simply believe and receive.**

"Amen" means "so be it." And that's what faith does - it agrees with what God has already said. When you speak "Amen" to His promises, you're not trying to convince God to act. You're aligning yourself with what He's already made available through Jesus.

This kind of assurance transforms your prayer life. You stop asking if God will come through, and you start declaring what He's already done. Faith responds to His "yes" with confident agreement, and your life becomes a testimony to His glory.

Reflection Questions:

Where are you still waiting for a "yes" from God where He's already said "yes" in Christ?

_____

_____

_____

_____

What promise are you declaring "Amen" to today?

_____

_____

_____

_____

Journal:

Write out a promise from God's Word that you've been unsure about and declare boldly, "In Christ, this promise is YES for me." Follow it with your own heartfelt "Amen."

_____

_____

_____

_____

_____

_____

_____

_____

_____

_____

_____

_____

_____

_____

_____

_____

_____

_____

YOU HAVE ACCESS

"For through Him we both have access by one Spirit to the Father."
- Ephesians 2:18 (NKJV)

You don't need a priest, a performance, or a perfect record to approach God. Because of your choice to follow Jesus, **you have direct access** - not to a distant deity, but to your Father. And this access isn't occasional or conditional - it's permanent and personal.

Through Christ, the veil has been torn. The separation is gone. You've been brought near by grace and welcomed into intimate fellowship. And the same Spirit who lives in you is the One who brings you straight to the heart of the Father.

This access means you don't have to wonder if God is listening. You don't have to qualify for His presence. **You are already in.** You have a seat at the table. You are welcome, wanted, and heard.

Whether you feel confident or weak, joyful or broken, you can come to the Father freely. And as you draw near, you won't find judgment - you'll find love, grace, and peace.

Reflection Questions:

Does your life reflect someone with full access to, if not what belief do you need to change?

_____

_____

_____

_____

_____

What does it mean for you today to draw near "by one Spirit to the Father"?

_____

_____

_____

Journal:

Write a prayer of gratitude for the access you've been given. Picture yourself stepping boldly into the Father's presence and write what you hear Him speaking back to your heart.

_____

_____

_____

_____

_____

_____

_____

_____

_____

_____

_____

_____

_____

_____

_____

_____

_____

_____

_____

YOU ARE A VITAL PART

"Now you [collectively] are Christ's body and [individually] you are members of it, each part severally and distinct - each with his own place and function." - 1 Corinthians 12:27 (AMPC)

You're not just in the Body of Christ - you are an essential, handpicked part of it. God didn't overlook you when He designed the Church. He didn't give you a generic calling or an accidental personality. You were created with a purpose, placed with intention, and gifted with something **only you** can bring.

In Christ's Body, there are no extras - only essentials. Whether your gift is seen or behind the scenes, big or small, dramatic or gentle - it matters. You matter.

This verse speaks to two truths: your unity with others in Christ and your distinct identity within that unity. You belong, **but you are not lost in the crowd.** God values your individuality and the unique function you carry.

Here's the grace: you don't have to try to be like anyone else. You just need to be faithful to the part He's called you to play. The more you embrace your God-given place, the more the Body functions in fullness.

Reflection Questions:

Do you believe you have a distinct role in the Body of Christ and if so, what do you think it is?

_____

_____

_____

_____

_____

_____

_____

_____

Are you comparing your place to others or celebrating the uniqueness of your own?

_____

_____

_____

_____

Journal:
Write a declaration of belonging: "I am a vital part of the Body of Christ." Ask God to show you the gifts He's placed in you and how to walk in them with boldness and joy.

_____

_____

_____

_____

_____

_____

_____

_____

_____

_____

_____

_____

_____

_____

_____

GOD IS FOR YOU

"What then shall we say to these things? If God is for us, who can be against us?" - Romans 8:31 (NKJV)

This question isn't asking for an answer - it's making a declaration. **God is for you**. Let that truth sink in. The Creator of heaven and earth, the One who knows the end from the beginning, the One who sent His Son for you, is on your side.

That means no enemy, no accusation, no mistake, no obstacle can successfully stand against you. It doesn't mean life will be free of opposition. It means no opposition can win. Why? Because the One who holds all power stands with you and in you.

When God is for you, you're never alone. You're never abandoned. You're never without help. He's not tolerating you. He's **championing** you. He's invested in your victory, your healing, your restoration, and your purpose.

Whatever you're facing today, you can look it in the eye and say, "You don't stand a chance because God is for me."

Reflection Questions:

Do you live with the awareness that God is for you, or are you still trying to earn His approval?

_____

_____

_____

_____

How would your mindset shift if you truly believed nothing and no one could stand against you?

_____

_____

_____

_____

Journal:

Write a declaration beginning with: "God is for me, so…" Fill it with faith, confidence, and truth. Let it become your battle cry in every circumstance.

_____

_____

_____

_____

_____

_____

_____

_____

_____

_____

_____

_____

_____

_____

_____

_____

_____

_____

_____

_____

_____

GREATER IS HE IN YOU

"You are of God, little children, and have overcome them, because He who is in you is greater than he who is in the world."
- 1 John 4:4 (NKJV)

You are not powerless. You are not outnumbered. You are not at the mercy of the world's chaos or the enemy's lies. Why? Because the **Greater One** lives inside of you.

This verse doesn't tell you to try to overcome It declares that you **have** overcome. And not by your strength, but because of who lives in you. The Holy Spirit - the same Spirit that raised Jesus from the dead - dwells in you, empowers you, and gives you victory.

The one who is in the world - the enemy, the culture, the pressure - is loud, but he is not greater. He may intimidate, but he cannot win. **Because the power in you is not just stronger. It is unmatched.**

You are of God. That means your identity, your authority, and your victory are already secured. You don't fight for victory. You fight **from** it, with the Greater One living in you every step of the way.

Reflection Questions:

What awareness do you have that the Greater One lives in you?

_____

_____

_____

_____

What fear or challenge do you need to confront today with the truth that He that is in you is greater?

_____

_____

_____

_____

_____

Journal:

Write a declaration starting with: "The One in me is greater than..." and list anything trying to oppose your peace, purpose, or identity. Declare victory from the inside out.

_____

_____

_____

_____

_____

_____

_____

_____

_____

_____

_____

_____

_____

_____

_____

_____

_____

_____

_____

_____

_____

_____

CAST IT ALL ON HIM

"Casting all your care upon Him, for He cares for you."
- 1 Peter 5:7 (NKJV)

God will never feel that you are taking advantage of Him. He wants you to come to Him rather than try and do it on your own. He doesn't just tolerate your burdens. He **invites** them. He's not asking you to carry your worries, anxieties, or fears with a brave face. He's asking you to **cast them** - throw them - fully onto Him, because **He cares for you**.

This verse is deeply personal. It's not a distant God offering a vague promise. It's your loving Father saying, "I see you, I care, let Me carry that." You were never designed to carry the weight of life on your own. Grace doesn't empower you to fake strength. It empowers you to rest in His.

Casting your care isn't a one-time act. It's a posture. It is a daily, sometimes moment-by-moment choice to release what you were never meant to manage and trust the One who holds all things together.

You don't have to hold it all together. He's already holding you.

Reflection Questions:

What burden have you been silently carrying that Jesus is asking you to cast on Him?

_____

_____

_____

_____

Do you believe He cares for *you*, not just the outcome?

_____

_____

_____

_____

Journal:

Write a letter to Jesus listing everything on your heart - the big, the small, the in-between. Then write this in bold: *"Jesus, I cast it all on You, because You care for me."*

_____

_____

_____

_____

_____

_____

_____

_____

_____

_____

_____

_____

_____

_____

_____

_____

_____

_____

STRENGTH FOR EVERY DAY

"I can do all things through Christ who strengthens me."
- Philippians 4:13 (NKJV)

This isn't just a motivational phrase. It's a powerful spiritual reality. Paul wrote these words not from a mountaintop, but from a prison cell. His strength wasn't circumstantial. It was **supernatural**.

You were never meant to live this life in your own ability. You were designed to be empowered by Christ Himself. His strength isn't just for emergencies. It's for **everything**: your calling, your parenting, your marriage, your waiting, your healing, your daily walk.

The secret is not in trying harder. It's in trusting deeper. Christ lives in you, and His power is made perfect in your weakness. You don't have to be enough, because He already is.

This verse doesn't promise ease. It promises empowerment. Whatever the season, whatever the struggle, whatever the assignment - you can do it, not because of your strength, but **through His**.

Reflection Questions:

Are there areas in your life where you've been relying on your own strength instead of Christ's?

_____

_____

_____

_____

What would it look like to truly depend on His power in your daily life?

_____

_____

_____

_____

Journal:

Write a declaration starting with: "Through Christ, I can…" and list everything you've been afraid to face or felt unqualified to do. Speak strength over every area by faith.

_____

_____

_____

_____

_____

_____

_____

_____

_____

_____

_____

_____

_____

_____

_____

_____

_____

_____

_____

YOU ARE HIS MASTERPIECE

"For we are His workmanship, created in Christ Jesus for good works, which God prepared beforehand that we should walk in them."
- Ephesians 2:10 (NKJV)

You are not a mistake, nor an accident. You are not random. **You are His workmanship** - His masterpiece - crafted with care, intention, and divine detail. The same God who spoke galaxies into existence handcrafted you in Christ for something **good**.

You weren't just saved **from** something. You were saved **for** something. God prepared works, assignments, encounters, moments of purpose for you before you even took your first breath, and they're not burdens. They're blessings. They're not to **prove** your worth - they flow **from** your worth.

When you embrace this truth, striving falls away. You stop trying to become something and begin to walk in what He already created you to be. You are not here to survive. You're here to thrive, shine, serve, and reflect the One who made you.

Every detail of your personality, story, and gifting fits into God's beautiful plan. You are not just useful. You are **uniquely designed**.

Reflection Questions:

What makes a masterpiece? How do you see yourself different from a masterpiece?

_____

_____

_____

_____

What "good works" has God placed in your heart that you've been hesitating to step into?

_____

_____

_____

Journal:
Write a declaration beginning with: "I am God's masterpiece..." and finish it by speaking truth over your value, purpose, and the unique impact you are called to make.

One Spirit with Him

"But he who is joined to the Lord becomes one spirit with him."
- 1 Corinthians 6:17 (ESV)

This isn't a metaphor. It's a miracle. When you said "yes" to Jesus, you weren't just forgiven. You were **joined** - fused together in spirit, no distance, no separation. You were made complete oneness with Christ Himself.

You are not just following Jesus. You are **in Him** and He is in you. That means His strength is your strength. His peace is your peace. His righteousness, His authority, and His rest are yours because you are one **spirit with Him**.

This changes everything about how you see yourself. You are not alone. You are not reaching for God. You are **united** with Him. And that union is not fragile. It's sealed by the Holy Spirit. Even when you feel weak, confused, or unworthy, the truth remains: you are joined to the Lord.

You don't have to "feel" close to God to be close. You are as close as spirit can get - **one with Him**. Let that truth settle deep in your soul.

Reflection Questions:

How is the truth of this verse different from what you have been believing or feeling?

_____

_____

_____

_____

How would your thoughts, prayers, or decisions change if you believed you were inseparably joined to the Lord?

_____

_____

_____

_____

Journal:

Write a declaration: "I am one spirit with the Lord." Let it become your meditation today, and especially in moments when you're tempted to feel far or disconnected.

_____

_____

_____

_____

_____

_____

_____

_____

_____

_____

_____

_____

_____

_____

_____

_____

_____

_____

_____

HE IS WORKING IT ALL FOR GOOD

"And we know that all things work together for good to those who love God, to those who are the called according to His purpose."
- **Romans 8:28 (NKJV)**

God doesn't waste anything. It does not mean that He is the cause or even instigator, but He is the Redeemer. He will redeem the waiting, the heartbreak, even the mistakes. This verse doesn't say all things are good. It says that in His hands, all things **have been redeemed for good**.

That means every piece of your story - the beautiful, the broken, the confusing - is being woven into a masterpiece by the One who sees the end from the beginning. You don't have to understand how. You just have to trust the **One who does**.

This promise is for those who love God and are called according to His purpose. That's you. You are called. You are loved. That means you can live with unshakable confidence, even when things don't look good yet, because your Redeemer is still working.

God doesn't just redeem moments. He redeems **people**. He's turning your life into a testimony of His faithfulness, one thread at a time.

Reflection Questions:

What situations in your life are you trusting God to work for good, even if you don't see it yet?

_____

_____

_____

_____

_____

_____

_____

How does believing this promise shift your perspective on the hard or hidden parts of your story?

_____

_____

_____

_____

_____

Journal:

Write a declaration of trust: "God, I believe You are working all things together for my good." Name any specific areas where you're choosing to trust His redemptive plan.

_____

_____

_____

_____

_____

_____

_____

_____

_____

_____

_____

_____

_____

_____

_____

YOU ARE CHOSEN TO SHINE

"But you are a chosen race, a royal priesthood, a dedicated nation, [God's] own purchased, special people, that you may set forth the wonderful deeds and display the virtues and perfections of Him Who called you out of darkness into His marvelous light."
- 1 Peter 2:9 (AMPC)

You are not forgotten. You are chosen. You are handpicked by God, not as an afterthought, but as part of His plan to reflect His light and glory to the world. You are royalty in His Kingdom, called to carry His presence and display His goodness wherever you go.

This verse reminds you that your identity isn't something you earn. It's something you **inherit**. You are God's own special possession, purchased with a price, set apart for something far greater than survival: to shine.

He called you out of darkness, not just to rescue you, but to reveal Himself through you. **You are a living display of His mercy, love, healing, and grace.** The transformation in your life is meant to be seen, not for your glory, but for His.

So walk tall today, not in pride, but in purpose. You are chosen. You are royal. You are anointed to proclaim and reflect the goodness of the One who brought you into the light.

Reflection Questions:

How does someone live who is chosen, royal, and set apart?

_____

_____

_____

_____

How can you display His light and love to those around you today?

_____

_____

_____

Journal:

Write a declaration: "I am chosen, royal, and called to shine." Thank God for calling you out of darkness and ask Him to use your life to reflect His marvelous light.

_____

_____

_____

_____

_____

_____

_____

_____

_____

_____

_____

_____

_____

_____

_____

_____

_____

_____

_____

_____

_____

JOY AND PEACE IN EVERY SEASON

"Rejoice in the Lord always; again I will say, rejoice. Let your reasonableness be known to everyone. The Lord is at hand; do not be anxious about anything, but in everything by prayer and supplication with thanksgiving let your requests be made known to God." - Philippians 4:4–6 (ESV)

Joy isn't circumstantial, it's relational. Paul commands us to **rejoice always**, not because everything always feels good, but because **God is, and will always be, near.** The key to peace in every situation isn't in controlling the outcome. It's in staying connected to the One who holds the outcome.

You're invited to **bring everything**, not just the polished prayers or the big crises, but every care, every concern, every unknown **to God.** You don't bring it in fear, but with **thanksgiving**, trusting that your Father already knows, already cares, and already has a plan.

This passage doesn't deny that anxiety exists. It simply tells you what to do with it: bring it to God, exchange it for peace, and root your heart in joy. Joy that isn't based on what changes around you, but on the One who never changes within you.

That's why you can release, rejoice, and rest, even in the middle of uncertainty.

Reflection Questions:

What have you been holding onto that God is inviting you to release through prayer?

_____

_____

_____

_____

_____

_____

How can you anchor your joy today in who He is, rather than in how things feel?

_____

_____

_____

_____

_____

_____

Journal:
Write a prayer of thanksgiving and surrender. Rejoice in who God is, thank Him in advance for what He's doing, and let your requests be made known, fully and freely.

_____

_____

_____

_____

_____

_____

_____

_____

_____

_____

_____

_____

_____

_____

CHOSEN, ADOPTED, ACCEPTED

"having predestined us to adoption as sons by Jesus Christ to Himself, according to the good pleasure of His will, to the praise of the glory of His grace, by which He made us accepted in the Beloved." - Ephesians 1:5–6 (NKJV)

Before you were even born, God had already chosen you, not out of obligation, but out of **delight**. He wanted you. He planned for you. Through Jesus, He adopted you into His family - not as a servant, but as a beloved child.

You are not barely welcomed into God's presence. You are **fully accepted**, not because of what you've done, but because of His grace. He placed you **in the Beloved**, clothed in Christ, covered by His righteousness, and sealed by His love.

This truth silences every whisper of rejection. It answers every wound that says you're not enough. You don't have to earn your place. You don't have to perform to be loved. You are already chosen, already adopted, and already accepted.

Let that truth wash over you today. You are not just tolerated by God. You are treasured by Him.

Reflection Questions:

How is God inviting you to release performance and receive His unconditional acceptance in a deeper way?

_____

_____

_____

How does knowing you've been adopted and chosen shift the way you relate to God?

_____

_____

_____

_____

Journal:
Write a letter to God thanking Him for choosing you before the foundation of the world. Declare: "I am accepted in the Beloved, and I belong."

_____

_____

_____

_____

_____

_____

_____

_____

_____

_____

_____

_____

_____

_____

_____

_____

_____

_____

_____

_____

WASHED, SANCTIFIED, JUSTIFIED

"Do you not know that the unrighteous will not inherit the kingdom of God? Do not be deceived. Neither fornicators, nor idolaters, nor adulterers, nor homosexuals, nor sodomites, nor thieves, nor covetous, nor drunkards, nor revilers, nor extortioners will inherit the kingdom of God. And such were some of you. But you were washed, you were sanctified, you were justified in the name of the Lord Jesus Christ and by the Spirit of our God."
- 1 Corinthians 6:9–11 (NKJV)

The emphasis in this passage isn't on who you were, but on what God has **done**. "Such were some of you" means your past is not your present. You are no longer defined by what once held you, but by the One who rescued, washed, and restored you.

You were **washed**, completely cleansed from sin and shame.

You were **sanctified**, set apart as holy, with a new purpose and identity.

You were **justified**, declared righteous, not by your works, but by Jesus' finished work on the cross. Justified means just if you have never, and now in right standing with God.

This isn't who you're trying to become. It's who you **already are** in Christ. You don't carry the labels of your past. You carry the name of Jesus. You are holy, forgiven, clean, and righteous, not because you earned it, but because grace made it yours.

So when the enemy tries to remind you of your past, remind him of your present: **washed, sanctified, justified**. Your life now reflects what Jesus has done, not what you once did.

Reflection Questions:

What old labels or lies you've been holding onto that God has already washed away?

_____

_____

_____

How can you walk more boldly today in the truth that you are sanctified and justified?

_____

_____

_____

_____

Journal:

Write a declaration beginning with: "I was, but now I am..." Let it be a line in the sand where grace rewrites your story and truth defines your identity.

_____

_____

_____

_____

_____

_____

_____

_____

_____

_____

_____

_____

_____

_____

_____

_____

His Spirit bears Witness

"The Spirit Himself bears witness with our spirit that we are children of God." - Romans 8:16 (NKJV)

You don't have to wonder if you belong to God. You don't have to second-guess your salvation or constantly seek proof of your place in His heart. The **Holy Spirit Himself** whispers to your spirit: **You are His**.

This isn't just a mental belief. It's a spiritual knowing deep within. The Spirit confirms what is true: **You are a child of God,** loved, chosen, secure not because you feel it every day, but because it's a truth sealed by the Spirit.

Even when doubts try to creep in, even when you stumble or feel distant, the Holy Spirit gently reminds you: "You're still Mine." His witness is greater than your feelings, stronger than your failures, and constant in every season.

Let this be your anchor. You don't have to strive to belong. You already do. You're not trying to become a child. You are one, by grace and through faith. The Spirit's voice is your reassurance, your security, your peace.

Reflection Questions:

What emotions or past experiences do you listen to more than the Spirit's witness?

_____

_____

_____

_____

How does knowing you are God's child affect the way you approach Him?

_____

_____

_____

_____

Journal:
Write a letter to your Heavenly Father from the heart of a confident child. Thank Him for the Spirit's voice in your life and ask Him to help you hear it more clearly each day.

_____

_____

_____

_____

_____

_____

_____

_____

_____

_____

_____

_____

_____

_____

_____

_____

_____

_____

_____

A Citizen of Heaven

"But our citizenship is in heaven, and from it we await a Savior, the Lord Jesus Christ." - **Philippians 3:20 (ESV)**

You may live on earth, but your **identity** is rooted in heaven. You're not just passing through life trying to survive. You're walking as a citizen of the Kingdom of God. That means your values, your mindset, and your hopes are shaped by heaven, not by the brokenness of this world.

This citizenship wasn't earned. **It was given.** The moment you believed in Jesus, your spiritual passport was issued and was sealed by the Holy Spirit. You now belong to a different realm, and your life reflects that higher reality.

While the world pulls toward fear, striving, and distraction, heaven calls you to peace, purpose, and focus on the eternal. You don't have to live weighed down by what's happening around you when you're anchored in the One who reigns above it all.

While you wait for Jesus to return, you wait with hope, not anxiety. He is your Savior, and your life is hidden in Him. **Everything** you do here matters, because you're representing your true home with every step you take.

Reflection Questions:

What earthly struggles have kept your focus instead of living from a heavenly perspective?

_____

_____

_____

_____

_____

_____

_____

What changes when you remember that your citizenship and your security is in heaven?

_____

_____

_____

_____

_____

Journal:

Write a declaration starting with: "I am a citizen of heaven..." and let it realign your heart with truth, hope, and eternal identity.

_____

_____

_____

_____

_____

_____

_____

_____

_____

_____

_____

_____

_____

_____

_____

_____

LIFE TO THE FULL

"The thief does not come except to steal, and to kill, and to destroy. I have come that they may have life, and that they may have it more abundantly."- **John 10:10 (NKJV)**

Jesus didn't come to offer survival. He came to offer **abundance**, a life that overflows with peace, purpose, joy, and intimacy with God. Abundant life isn't about outward circumstances. It's about inward fullness. It's the deep, settled assurance that because you have Him, you have **everything** you need.

The enemy's strategy is always the same: steal your joy, kill your confidence, and destroy your identity. But Jesus came to reverse it all. In Him you are protected, provided for, and fully alive.

This isn't a promise for **someday**. It's for today. You can live in the fullness of Christ right now, in every area of life: spiritually, emotionally, and relationally. Abundant life means walking in freedom, knowing you're loved, and fulfilling the purpose He created you for.

Don't settle for less than what Jesus paid for. You were made for more than just getting by. You were made to thrive in His love and truth.

Reflection Questions:

In what areas in your life have you've settled for less than abundance?

_____

_____

_____

_____

_____

_____

_____

_____

What would it look like to receive and walk in the fullness Jesus promised you?

_____

_____

_____

_____

Journal:

Write a declaration: "Jesus, I receive the abundant life You came to give me..." and list the areas where you're believing for His fullness to overflow.

_____

_____

_____

_____

_____

_____

_____

_____

_____

_____

_____

_____

_____

_____

_____

_____

WALKING IN AUTHORITY

"Behold, I give you the authority to trample on serpents and scorpions, and over all the power of the enemy, and nothing shall by any means hurt you." - Luke 10:19 (NKJV)

Jesus didn't just save you. He empowered you. He gave you authority. You are not weak, helpless, or at the mercy of darkness. You carry delegated power from the King of Kings to stand, speak, and walk in victory.

Serpents and scorpions represent every evil force, lie, and attack and even sickness that would try to stop your forward movement. But Jesus says you have **authority over all of it** - not just some – but all.

This isn't about hype or fear. It's about **identity**. Authority doesn't come from shouting louder or doing more. It comes from knowing who you are and whose name you carry. And when you know you've been given authority, you stop tolerating what Jesus already defeated.

You don't have to fight for power. **You already have it.** Nothing the enemy throws at you can truly harm you when you're walking in the truth of your position in Christ.

Reflection Questions:

Where in your life have you felt intimidated or hesitant - and how is God calling you to rise up in the authority He's already given you?

_____

_____

_____

_____

_____

_____

_____

_____

How might your thoughts, prayers, or actions change if you fully stood in your God-given authority in this season?

_____

_____

_____

_____

_____

_____

Journal:

Write a bold declaration: "In Jesus' name, I walk in authority ..." and finish the sentence with every area where you're taking back ground from fear, lies, or defeat.

_____

_____

_____

_____

_____

_____

_____

_____

_____

_____

_____

_____

_____

BLESSED WITH EVERY SPIRITUAL BLESSING

"Blessed be the God and Father of our Lord Jesus Christ, who has blessed us with every spiritual blessing in the heavenly places in Christ." - Ephesians 1:3 (NKJV)

You're not waiting to be blessed. You already are. God isn't holding out on you. **In Christ, He has given you every spiritual blessing.** That means nothing is missing - nothing is lacking. You have access to everything you need to live a victorious, grace-filled, Spirit-led life.

These blessings aren't limited to what you can see or touch. They are **heavenly, eternal, and powerful.** Things like righteousness, peace, joy, wisdom, authority, identity, and purpose. These are your inheritance, not because of your performance, but because you are in Christ.

This verse shifts your perspective from begging to believing. You don't need to strive for what's already yours. You need to **receive it by faith.** You're not chasing after God's favor. **You're living from it.**

Let your heart rest in the truth that your Father has already equipped and empowered you with everything heaven has to offer through Jesus.

Reflection Questions:

How do you change living from the mindset of someone still waiting to be blessed to one who is already blessed?

_____

_____

_____

_____

_____

_____

_____

_____

What blessings in Christ have you been overlooking or underestimating?

_____

_____

_____

_____

_____

Journal:

Write a declaration: "In Christ, I am blessed with…" and list the spiritual blessings you're choosing to recognize and walk in today.

_____

_____

_____

_____

_____

_____

_____

_____

_____

_____

_____

_____

_____

_____

_____

_____

RESURRECTION POWER LIVES IN YOU

"But if the Spirit of Him who raised Jesus from the dead dwells in you, He who raised Christ from the dead will also give life to your mortal bodies through His Spirit who dwells in you." - Romans 8:11 (NKJV)

The same Spirit who raised Jesus from the dead lives in you. Think about that. Resurrection power isn't far off, reserved for a distant miracle. **It's dwelling within you right now.**

This means you are not spiritually weak or empty. You are a carrier of divine life - life that revives, restores, empowers, and overcomes. This power isn't just for eternity. It's for **today**. It gives life to your **mortal body**. This is your everyday reality: strength when you're tired, hope when you're weary, healing where there's brokenness.

You don't need to stir up power. You need to **recognize** and **release** what's already inside you. The Spirit of God isn't visiting you. He **dwells** in you – constant, unshakable, overflowing.

This is the reality of life in Christ: you are alive with the very power that broke death's grip. Let that shape how you live, pray, speak, and believe.

Reflection Questions:

What is the evidence that resurrection power is alive and active in your life today?

_____

_____

_____

_____

Where do you need to see that life-giving power move in your body, mind, emotions, or circumstances?

_____

_____

_____

_____

Journal:

Write a declaration: "The Spirit of God lives in me, and His resurrection power gives life to..." and finish with every area you're believing to see renewed and restored.

_____

_____

_____

_____

_____

_____

_____

_____

_____

_____

_____

_____

_____

_____

_____

_____

_____

_____

_____

_____

_____

_____

No Condemnation – Only Freedom

"There is therefore now no condemnation for those who are in Christ Jesus. For the law of the Spirit of life has set you free in Christ Jesus from the law of sin and death." - Romans 8:1–2 (ESV)

*If you are in Christ. And if you are, then **there is no condemnation for you**. There is none, not a trace, not from God, not from your past, and not from yourself. Jesus didn't just save you from sin. He set you free from the **weight** and **judgment** of it.*

The enemy wants you to live in guilt, but God invites you to live in grace. Condemnation says, "You're still not enough," but grace says, "You're already accepted." The Spirit of life has broken the old system - the law of sin and death - and now you are governed by freedom, not fear.

This doesn't mean you'll never make mistakes. It means that when you do, you can run to your Father with boldness, not shame. You don't have to earn your way back into God's presence. You never left it.

*You're not just forgiven. You're **free**, and that freedom is your new normal.*

Reflection Questions:

What condemnation are you still carrying that Jesus already paid to remove?

_____

_____

_____

_____

_____

_____

_____

_____

How would your life look different if you fully believed you were free?

_____

_____

_____

_____

_____

Journal:

Write a declaration starting with: "There is no condemnation for me…" and let the truth of your freedom in Christ break off every chain of guilt, shame, or striving.

_____

_____

_____

_____

_____

_____

_____

_____

_____

_____

_____

_____

_____

_____

ABIDE AND BEAR FRUIT

"I am the vine; you are the branches. Whoever abides in me and I in him, he it is that bears much fruit, for apart from me you can do nothing." - John 15:5 (ESV)

Your strength, your growth, and your fruitfulness don't come from doing, they come from **abiding**. Jesus didn't ask you to produce fruit on your own. He invited you to remain in Him, because He is your source. The vine never asks the branch to perform, only to stay connected.

Abiding isn't about doing more. It's about staying close. It's about living from the awareness that Christ is in you, and you are in Him. As you remain in His presence, His life flows through you, bringing peace where there was pressure, joy where there was heaviness, and power where there was weakness.

When you try to produce apart from Him, burnout follows. But when you abide, fruit happens naturally. Love, peace, patience, boldness, creativity, strength, these grow as a result of staying connected to the Vine.

You were never meant to do life alone. You were made to abide in the One who already finished the work and now invites you to rest and grow in Him.

Reflection Questions:

How have you been trying to bear fruit in your own strength instead of staying connected to Jesus?

_____

_____

_____

_____

_____

_____

_____

What does abiding look like for you in this season?

_____

_____

_____

_____

_____

Journal:
Write a prayer of surrender and connection: "Jesus, I choose to abide in You..." Ask Him to teach you to live from the Vine and trust Him to bring fruit in every area of your life.

_____

_____

_____

_____

_____

_____

_____

_____

_____

_____

_____

_____

_____

_____

_____

_____

_____

Rivers of Living Water

"Whoever believes in me, as the Scripture has said, 'Out of his heart will flow rivers of living water.'" - **John 7:38 (ESV)**

Believing in Jesus doesn't just bring life to you. It brings life **through** you. The moment you believed, the Holy Spirit came to dwell in you, not as a trickle, but as a river - a continual, powerful flow of God's presence, power, and grace.

This river isn't meant to be contained. It's meant to **overflow** into your thoughts, your conversations, your prayers, and your impact. You are not a dry well. You are a living fountain. The more you remain connected to Jesus, the more that river flows effortlessly.

This isn't about trying harder to be spiritual. It's about **believing** and **letting** the Spirit move through your surrendered life. When you yield to Him, the flow of living water refreshes you and becomes a source of life for others.

Don't underestimate what's inside of you. His Spirit is active, alive, ready to flow. Let Him move. Let Him speak. Let Him heal, encourage, and overflow through you to others today.

Reflection Questions:

How does the life of someone who has the river of living water flowing from them differ to someone who has not experienced it?

_____

_____

_____

_____

How can you open your heart more fully today and let that living water flow to others?

_____

_____

_____

_____

Journal:

Write a prayer of invitation: "Holy Spirit, flow through me like a river..." Ask Him to refresh your heart and to pour out His love, grace, and truth through your life.

_____

_____

_____

_____

_____

_____

_____

_____

_____

_____

_____

_____

_____

_____

_____

_____

_____

_____

_____

Final Note

Thank you for walking this journey with me. My prayer is that, through each verse, reflection, and quiet moment with the Holy Spirit, you've encountered more of the truth about who you are, and even more importantly, who He is in you.

You were never meant to live striving for identity or acceptance. You are fully known by the One who created you, and fully free because of what Jesus has done. That truth doesn't change with your feelings or circumstances. It is your unshakable foundation.

As you go forward, keep growing in grace. Keep choosing truth over lies, and keep coming back to the Word, where your identity is anchored, and your confidence is renewed. The journey doesn't end here. It continues in every step of faith, every moment of surrender, and every act of bold obedience.

If this devotional has impacted your life in any way, I would be honored to hear your story. You can reach me at booksbyjeannine@gmail.com. Your testimony may encourage someone else to step into freedom too.

You are loved. You are chosen. You are complete in Him.

With love and grace,

Jeannine

Made in the USA
Middletown, DE
10 May 2025

75355120R00070